ICEBERGS & GLACIERS

SEYMOUR SIMON

Updated Edition

HARPER

An Imprint of HarperCollinsPublishers

In memory of Charles Swithinbank, an esteemed glaciologist at Cambridge University, who graciously met with me and allowed many of his photographs to be used in the first edition of Icebergs & Glaciers.

Special thanks to Robert Byrne

Photo Credits

Page 2: © Bryan and Cherry Alexander / Science Source; page 4: © British Antarctic Survey / Science Source; page 6: © Don Komarechka / Science Source; page 7: © Frans Lanting / MINT Images / Science Source; page 8: © Georg Gerster / Science Source; page 11: © Science Source; page 12: © Mario Tama / Getty Images; page 13: © NASA/Studinger; page 15: © Science Source; page 16: © David Nunuk / Science Source; page 17: © Frans Lanting / MINT Images / Science Source; pages 18, top to bottom: © Dr Juerg Alean / Science Source; © Tom McHugh / Science Source; page 19: © Science Source; page 20: © Dr. Juerg Alean / Science Source; page 21: © William Bacon / Science Source; page 23: © Science Source; page 24: © Science Source; page 27: © Michael S. Nolan; page 28: © NASA / Goddard Space Flight Center; page 29: © Steve Allen / Science Source; page 30: © D. P. Burnside / Science Source.

Library of Congress Control Number: 2017939003
ISBN 978-0-06-247039-3 (trade bdg.)—ISBN 978-0-06-247038-6 (pbk.)

17 18 19 20 21 SCP 10 9 8 7 6 5 4 3 2 1
❖
Revised edition, 2018

Author's Note

From a young age, I was interested in animals, space, my surroundings—all the natural sciences. When I was a teenager, I became the president of a nationwide junior astronomy club with a thousand members. After college, I became a classroom teacher for nearly twenty-five years while also writing articles and books for children on science and nature even before I became a full-time writer. My experience as a teacher gives me the ability to understand how to reach my young readers and get them interested in the world around us.

I've written more than 300 books, and I've thought a lot about different ways to encourage interest in the natural world, as well as how to show the joys of nonfiction. When I write, I use comparisons to help explain unfamiliar ideas, complex concepts, and impossibly large numbers. I try to engage your senses and imagination to set the scene and to make science fun. For example, in *Penguins*, I emphasize the playful nature of these creatures on the very first page by mentioning how penguins excel at swimming and diving. I use strong verbs to enhance understanding. I make use of descriptive detail and ask questions that anticipate what you may be thinking (sometimes right at the start of the book).

Many of my books are photo-essays, which use extraordinary photographs to amplify and expand the text, creating different and engaging ways of exploring nonfiction. You'll also find a glossary, an index, and website and research recommendations in most of my books, which make them ideal for enhancing your reading and learning experience. As William Blake wrote in his poem, I want my readers "to see a world in a grain of sand, / And a heaven in a wild flower, / Hold infinity in the palm of your hand, / And eternity in an hour."

Seymour Simon

For most of us, spring means the return of warm weather. Snow melts, and frozen lakes and rivers thaw. The icy scenes of winter begin to disappear.

But some places remain cold all year round. This photo was taken at midnight during the middle of summer in Antarctica. At that time of year, the sun never sets during the night but remains low in the sky.

Antarctica is always covered by deep layers of ice and snow. So, too, are parts of Greenland, Canada, Alaska, and Iceland. Even during summers, ice and snow still cover about one-tenth of Earth's land surface.

The upper slopes and peaks of high mountains all over the world are also covered by ice and snow. These places of everlasting snow are said to be above the snow line. Summertime snowfields are found in the Rockies, the Himalayas, the Alps, the Andes, and even at the equator high atop Mount Kilimanjaro. It is in the constantly cold lands and above the snow line that glaciers are born.

A single snowflake is a feathery crystal of ice about the size of your fingernail. Every snowflake is six-sided, yet each has a different shape.

Once the spinning flakes fall to the ground, they begin to clump together and lose their pointed beauty. Soon the snowflakes become rounded grains of ice with tiny bubbles of air trapped inside. As more snow falls, the weight of the snow and ice squeezes the grains of ice together, forcing out the trapped air. The color of the ice begins to change, too. The white of airy snow becomes the steel blue of airless ice. Finally, the blue ice crystals begin to pack together into a solid field of ice.

Greenland glacier

As more snow falls, the **ice field** becomes thicker and heavier, pressing downward with great force against the ground. As years go by, the ice field grows until it is about sixty feet deep. Then something strange happens.

The huge mass of ice begins to move. The ice bends and cracks and starts to slide over the ground, moving downhill. The ice moves slowly, usually less than two feet a day and sometimes only an inch or two. But however slowly, when an ice field begins to move, it has become a **glacier**.

Glaciers are sometimes called rivers of ice, but a glacier moves differently than a river. Water flows freely, but ice is hard and can crack easily. For many years, scientists called **glaciologists** have studied how glaciers move. Some of their early findings were accidental. In 1827, one Swiss scientist built a hut on an Alpine glacier. When he returned three years later, he found that the hut had moved more than one hundred yards downhill.

In recent years, scientists have found that glaciers move in two different ways. One way is by sliding across the ground on a very thin film of water from melted ice. This **meltwater**, sometimes only the thickness of a sheet of paper, allows the ice to slide more easily.

The second way that a glacier moves is called creep. The tremendous weight of the glacier makes the crystals of ice slowly form layers one atop another. Then the layers begin gliding or creeping over one another.

All glaciers move in both ways. But some glaciers move more by sliding over the ground, while others move more by creeping. The photograph shows the Byrd Glacier in Antarctica. Antarctic glaciers move mostly by creeping.

Byrd Glacier, Antarctica

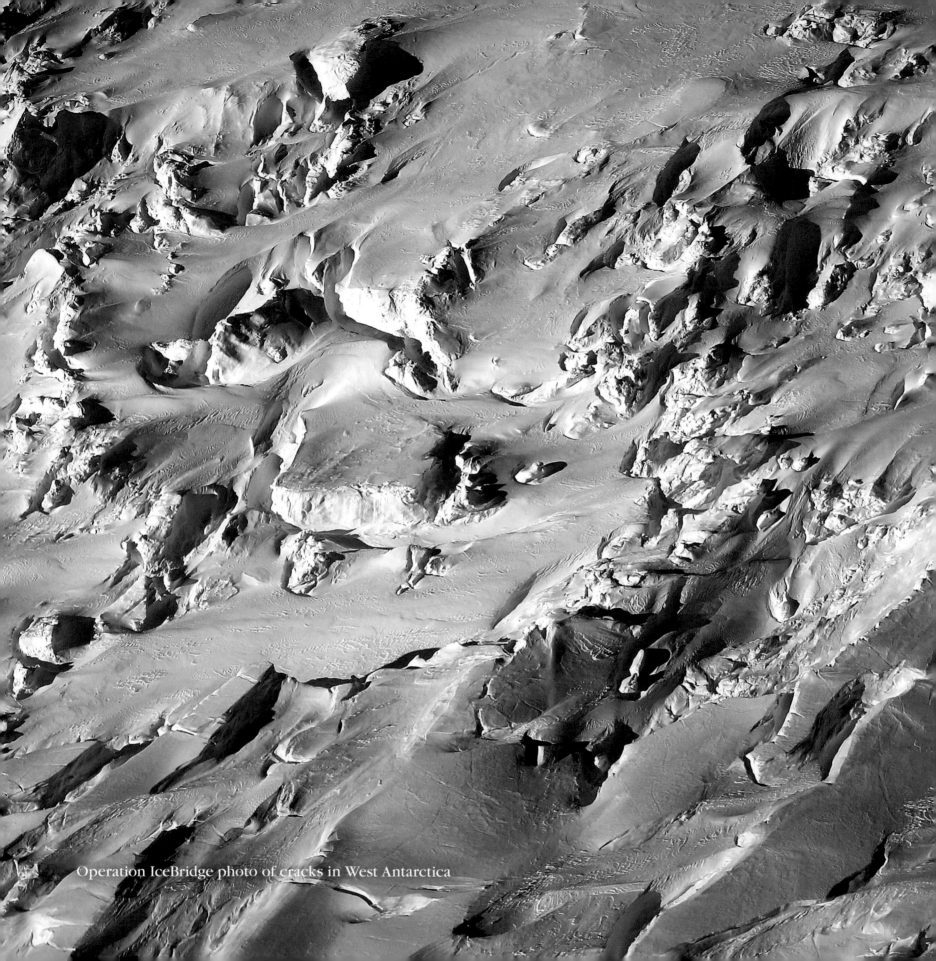
Operation IceBridge photo of cracks in West Antarctica

Different parts of a glacier move at different speeds. Louis Agassiz, a nineteenth-century Swiss-American naturalist and scientist, once planted rows of stakes in straight lines across a glacier. The following year Agassiz found that the stakes had all moved down the valley. But the stakes in the middle of the glacier had moved the farthest. That showed that the ice in the middle of the glacier was moving faster than the ice along the sides.

In the early part of the twentieth century, Swiss and Italian scientists drilled holes straight down through the thickness of a glacier. Then they placed iron rods in the holes. Over the years, the scientists found that the rods bent at the top. This showed that the ice at the top of a glacier moves more quickly than the ice at the bottom.

In 2009, NASA began Operation IceBridge, flying missions using airplanes equipped with modern instruments for measuring annual changes in thickness and movement of sea ice, glaciers, and **ice sheets**. This image, taken from an Operation IceBridge plane, shows ice cracks near the coast of West Antarctica. Scientists say that IceBridge data show that the West Antarctic ice sheet is melting each year and is directly contributing to rising sea levels all over the world.

The thicker the glacier, the faster it moves. That's because the greater weight of the glacier causes the crystals of ice to creep more rapidly. Also, a steep glacier will flow much more quickly than one on level land.

Temperature is a third factor that affects the speed of a glacier. The warmer the glacier, the faster the ice moves because there is a greater amount of meltwater beneath the ice. In fact, scientists sometimes group glaciers together depending on whether they are cold or warm. But even "warm" glaciers are still mostly frozen.

Some glaciers move so slowly that you might not notice their motion for a long time. The cold Alaskan glaciers in this satellite photo creep downhill at only about six inches per *year*. But there are some steep, warm glaciers that flow more than one hundred feet a *day*.

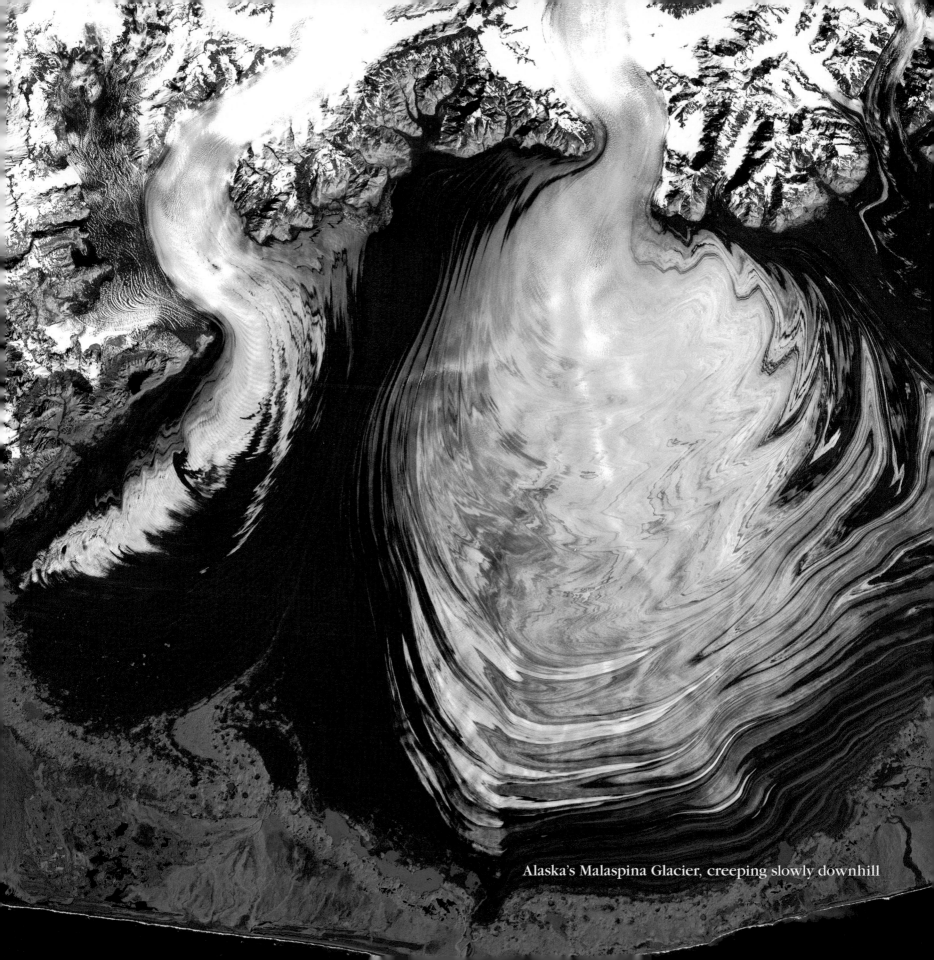

Alaska's Malaspina Glacier, creeping slowly downhill

As the glacier moves, the ice on top bends and sometimes cracks. The cracks in the ice are called **crevasses**. The crevasses can be deep and wide and very dangerous for people exploring the glacier.

When glaciers move, they grind and crush everything in their path. Small stones and huge rocks are pulled from the ground and carried along. Slowly, but with irresistible force, glaciers cut and carve the land. Trees, forests, hills, and even mountains are ground down over the years. The photo above shows how most of the mountain has been carried away by the ice, leaving sharp peaks and ragged ridges.

As glaciers move, they often scratch lines into the layers of rock that lie beneath the soil, as shown in the photo above. The scratches are made by smaller rocks carried along by the ice.

Sometimes glaciers wear down the bedrock to smooth, rounded humps. To some people, these rocks have the shape of a flock of grazing sheep. So they are called ***roches moutonnées***, French words that translate loosely to mean "sheep rocks," as shown in the photo below.

The rocks carried along by a glacier are broken down and ground into smaller and smaller pieces. The smaller pieces are ground again and again until they

are very tiny particles, almost too small for you to see. These particles, called **rock flour**, are carried away by a glacier's meltwater. The rock flour carried by the meltwater stream from a glacier turns the seawater a grayish-brown color, as shown in the image on the right.

Bigger than most mountain glaciers are **ice caps**—mountain glaciers that have become so thick that the mountain is almost buried. Ice caps are sheets of ice covering thousands of square miles. They form in **polar** and **subpolar regions** that are high in elevation and fairly flat.

Iceland's largest ice cap covers more than three thousand square miles. There is an active volcano buried beneath the western part of that ice cap. The heat from the volcano is always melting the ice above, forming a huge **reservoir** of meltwater. Every five years or so, the meltwater bursts out from under an edge of the cap. The roaring waters carry large boulders and giant blocks of ice. For miles around, the land is flooded and becomes a vast lake.

Iceland, just below the Arctic Circle, is warming up very quickly this century, about four times as fast as the Northern Hemisphere average. The three hundred plus glaciers that cover 10 percent of the land are losing an average of eleven billion tons of ice in a single year. That is enough to fill fifty large water trucks every minute for a year. Some of the glaciers have already vanished, and others will be gone in a decade. Climate change is affecting glaciers all over the world.

Ice sheets are the largest kind of glaciers. The Antarctic ice sheet is the biggest in the world. It is larger than the United States, Mexico, and Central America combined. In some places, the Antarctic ice sheet is more than fifteen thousand feet thick. That's about the height of ten Empire State Buildings stacked one atop another. Where an ice sheet meets the sea, it forms an **ice shelf** over the water.

Large masses of ice often break away from glaciers or ice shelves. The glacier is said to be calving, and the floating blocks of ice are called **icebergs**. Calving happens more rapidly as the world undergoes global warming. As an iceberg floats, it melts, changes shape, and breaks apart. Until an iceberg melts and disappears completely, most of it is underwater.

The photo shows the northern edge of a giant iceberg named B-15A, a remnant of Iceberg B-15. The giant iceberg broke away from the Ross Ice Shelf in Antarctica. Iceberg B-15 was the largest iceberg ever measured, hundreds of feet high, around 183 miles long and 23 miles wide, with a surface area of 4,200 square miles—bigger than the states of Delaware and Rhode Island put together. Researchers use global positioning systems (GPS), weather monitoring stations, and seismometers to track giant icebergs. The goal is to learn more about what causes giant icebergs to calve, how and why they drift, what happens when the icebergs warm, and why they produce earthquake-like shaking. Some of these iceberg quakes are tracked thousands of miles away.

Only a small part of an iceberg shows above the water. About seven-eighths of the "berg" is hidden beneath the waves because glacial ice is only slightly lighter than an equal amount of seawater. The large, unseen part of an iceberg adds to the danger of a collision with a nearby ship.

On the night of April 14, 1912, the *Titanic*, the "safest ship in the world" according to its builders, was steaming across the North Atlantic. Yet in a few hours the ship had gone to the bottom of the ocean after striking a large iceberg. More than fifteen hundred people died in the icy waters that night. The next year, the International Ice Patrol was established, and it is still on the job. The patrol searches for dangerous icebergs and helps ships avoid them. Yet in 2007, a cruise ship, the MS *Explorer*, hit submerged ice off Antarctica and sank. Fortunately, all 154 passengers and crew were safely picked up by a passing cruise ship.

Icebergs someday may prove to be useful as a source of freshwater for dry lands. One plan calls for mile-long Antarctic icebergs to be towed to distant countries by powerful tugboats and helicopters. The icebergs would be wrapped with layers of plastic insulation to protect them from melting on their journey. But there are still many problems with this idea, and it may be years, if ever, before icebergs are transported in this way.

1980

2012

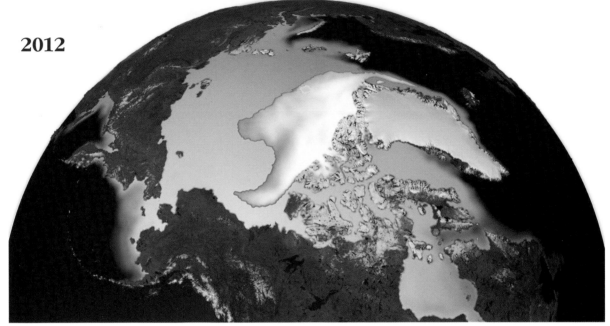

Twenty thousand years ago, ice sheets covered most of Canada, all of New England, and much of the midwestern and northwestern United States. Most of Great Britain and large parts of the Soviet Union, Germany, and Poland, along with smaller parts of Austria, Italy, and France, were also covered by ice.

Then, about ten thousand years ago, the ice began to melt. Today glaciers are found only in cold polar regions and on high mountains.

As glaciers and ice sheets melt at an increasing rate, they contribute to a rise in the sea level. Sea levels rose more than five inches in the last century, more than any time in the previous twenty-eight hundred years. While a few inches may not sound like a lot, higher sea levels result in increased flooding during storms and at high tide. Scientists say that melting ice due to climate change could raise global sea levels almost two feet by the end of this century, and more than six feet in another hundred years.

Glacially deposited boulders in Wisconsin, USA

Today we can see the ways that the land was changed by the glaciers. The rivers of ice cut valleys through the land and made rolling hills. Rocks and boulders were dragged from one place and dropped in other places far away.

Perhaps where you live now was once covered by ice. If you look around, you may find clues to past ice ages: scratches in bedrock, a big boulder that stands alone, a round pond left behind as the ice melted. Some scientists say that the last century has been the warmest in the past four thousand years, and it may become even warmer in the next century. Will this mean the end of ice ages? Many mysteries about climate and ice remain. Scientists continue to study past ice ages, and ice sheets and glaciers of today. And little by little, the world of ice is yielding its secrets to science.

GLOSSARY

Avalanche—A great mass of snow and ice or dirt and rocks that suddenly plunges down a mountainside.

Crevasse—A deep crack in the thick ice of a glacier or the ground.

Glacier—A huge mass of ice that slowly moves down a mountain or over land.

Glaciologist—Scientist who studies glaciers and ice sheets.

Iceberg—A large mass of ice floating in the ocean.

Ice cap—A covering of ice over a large area of land, such as in Iceland.

Ice field—A large mass of ice on land that forms from accumulation of snow.

Ice sheet—Very large mass of glacier ice covering polar landscapes.

Ice shelf—A large, flat mass of floating ice in polar regions.

Meltwater—Water formed from the melting of ice and snow, especially from a glacier.

Moraine—A large mass of earth and rocks carried and then deposited by a glacier when it melts.

Polar regions—Large areas around Earth's North or South Poles.

Reservoir—A large volume of water stored in one place.

Roches moutonnées—Outcrops of rocks shaped by the passage of glaciers into the form of rounded rocks. The words come from the French, meaning, "fleecy rocks," looking like the backs of sheep.

Rock flour—Finely powdered rock formed by the grinding action of a glacier.

Subpolar region—The area next to a polar region that has climates of usually long, very cold winters and short, cool to mild summers.

INDEX

READ MORE ABOUT IT

Seymour Simon's website
www.seymoursimon.com

NASA's Climate Kids
climatekids.nasa.gov/menu/
weather-and-climate

Weather & Atmosphere Education
www.noaa.gov/
weather-atmosphere/education

National Weather Service
www.weather.gov

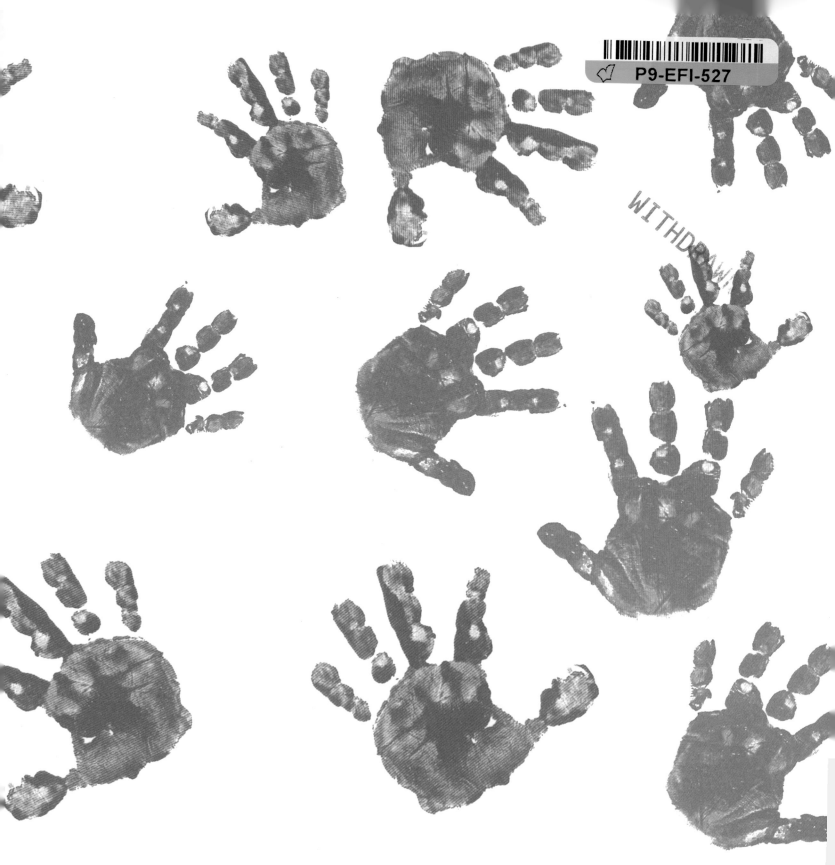

P9-EFI-527

Rolling Along

The Story of Taylor and His Wheelchair

The Rehabilitation Institute of Chicago Learning Book Series

FROM THE THE WESLEY M. AND SUZANNE S. DIXON EDUCATION AND TRAINING CENTER

The Making of My Special Hand: Madison's Story
Rolling Along: The Story of Taylor and His Wheelchair

To my loving parents, Jack and Joyce Riggio, for the love and guidance they give to me daily. I love you.

Special Thanks
To Taylor and Tyler and their parents, Twana and Jeffery, for graciously allowing me to share a wonderful piece of their life with others.
To Kathryn Danian, physical therapist, for her patience during the countless moments I interfered with Taylor's therapy sessions;
and to Camille, Michael, Alex, and Grant for their participation in the book.
To my husband, Bobby, for encouraging me to reach my personal goals, and to my three beautiful children, Dominic, Grant, and Gianna.

—J. R. H.

Ω
Published by
PEACHTREE PUBLISHERS, LTD.
1700 Chattahoochee Avenue
Atlanta, GA 30318-2112

www.peachtree-online.com

Book design by Nicola Simmonds and Matthew Carmack
Original photography by Jamee Riggio Heelan

Printed in Singapore

10 9

Library of Congress Cataloging-in-Publication Data
Heelan, Jamee Riggio.
    Rolling along : the story of Taylor and his wheelchair / Jamee Riggio Heelan ;
illustrated by Nicola Simmonds.–1st ed.
        p. cm.
    Summary: Explains how having cerebral palsy affects Taylor, and how getting a wheelchair makes a big difference in helping him get around, do things by himself, and even play basketball with his twin Tyler.
    ISBN 13: 978-1-56145-219-4 / ISBN 10: 1-56145-219-X
    1. Cerebral palsy–Juvenile literature. 2. Cerebral palsied children–Juvenile literature. [1. Cerebral palsy. 2. Wheelchairs.] I. Simmonds, Nicola, ill. II. Title.

RJ496.C4 H44 2000
616.8'36–dc21   99-087580

A Rehabilitation Institute of Chicago Learning Book

Rolling Along

*The Story of Taylor
and His Wheelchair*

Jamee Riggio Heelan, OTR/L
Rehabilitation Institute of Chicago

Illustrations by Nicola Simmonds

PEACHTREE
ATLANTA

Hi. My name is Taylor. I have a twin

brother, Tyler, who looks a

lot like me. He's also

my best friend.

We both like to eat chocolate ice cream, wrestle with each other, and watch the Chicago Bulls play basketball. We both like to read about dinosaurs.

But unlike Tyler, I was born with cerebral palsy. That's what my doctor calls my condition. It causes my brain (the cerebral part) to tell my muscles to jump (the palsy part) instead of moving smoothly.

Tyler can run, jump, and skip, but because I have cerebral palsy, it's hard for me to walk.

For a long time I've used braces on my legs and a walker to help me move. Every week I visit a physical therapist named Kathryn. She stretches my muscles and then helps me practice balancing and working my muscles.

I have lots of friends in therapy. Some of them use braces or wheelchairs because like me, they have never been able to get around without special equipment. Others are in therapy because they were in accidents. Some can't move their arms or legs at all. We're all in therapy to get stronger.

Kathryn taught me how to use
my walker, which helped me
walk on my own two feet.
I could go short distances by myself
with it, but I moved very slowly
and got tired easily.

When I went to and from therapy,
my mom had to carry me.
Sometimes I got frustrated
because I had to depend on
other people so much.

When Kathryn let me try using a wheelchair in therapy, I was so excited. Tyler pushed me around in it because it was hard for me to get it to move on my own.

At first I thought I would roll in the wheelchair as fast as I wanted and that moving around would be easy. But I had to practice a lot. I had to make my arms strong and learn how to roll the wheelchair back and forth, how to turn, and how to use the brakes to stop the wheelchair from rolling.

One of my school friends felt sorry for me when he heard I was getting a wheelchair. He thought that even though it took me a long time to move with my walker, getting around on my own two feet was better than rolling along in a wheelchair.

I told him I can still use my walker for short distances. But now I won't always get so tired and I won't have to be carried. Now I'll be able to move on my own. Then my friend was as happy as I was.

One day, Mom and Dad and Tyler brought me to therapy for a big surprise. My new wheelchair had come in! It was bright red and blue, with thick tires. I was so excited. I knew I would be able to get around faster in a wheelchair than I could with my walker.

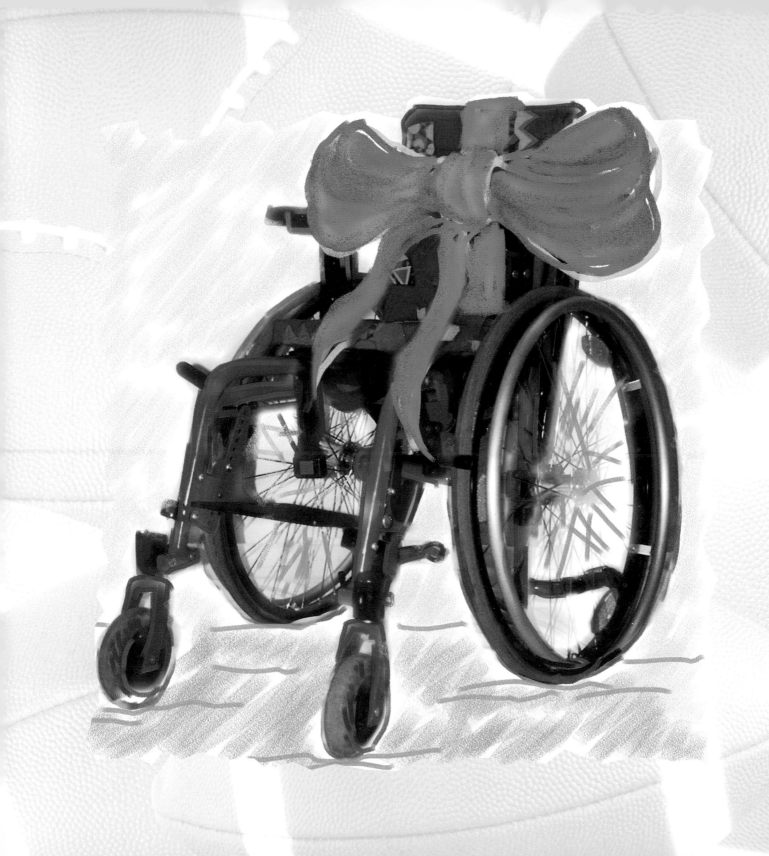

Now I can turn to the right and left and I'm even learning how to "pop a wheelie," which means making the wheelchair's front wheels pop up in the air. That way I can get over bumps or big cracks in the sidewalk.

Tyler helps me practice wheelies by pulling back on my wheelchair handles and stepping on the lower bar. This lifts up the front of the chair a little. Then I balance myself in the chair and try to get over the bump. When I'm a little bigger and stronger I'll be able to pop a wheelie all by myself.

Now I need to pay attention to things that people who aren't in wheelchairs don't have to worry about. If a building has stairs at the front entrance and no ramp, I can't roll myself up to the door. If its heavy front doors don't open with a button, I can't go inside. If the building has stairs or an escalator inside and no elevator, I can't get to the other floors.

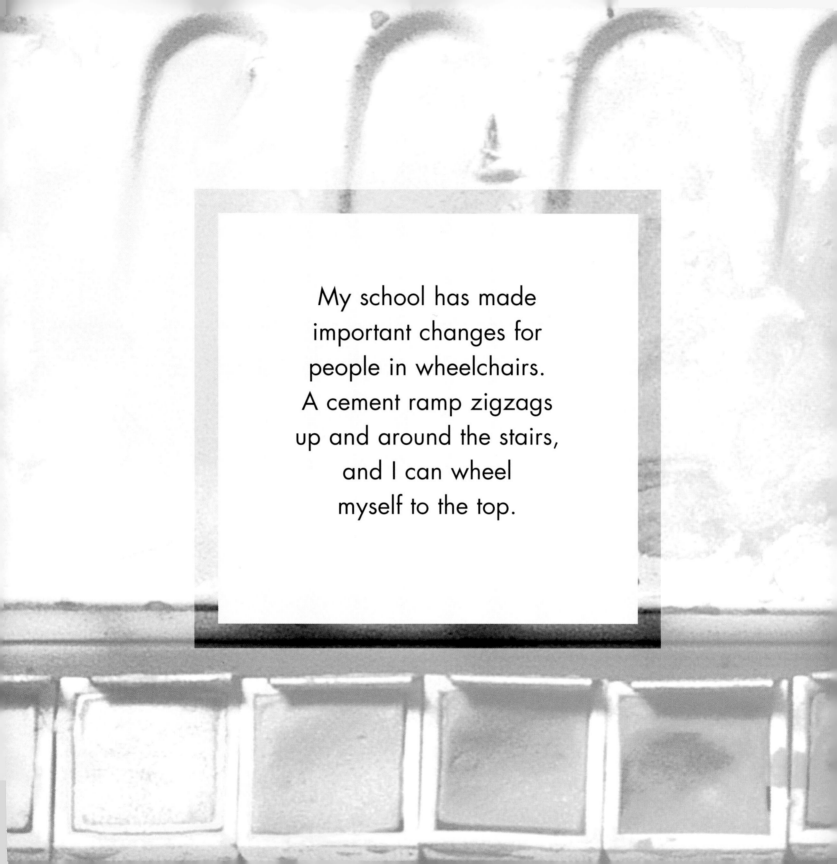

My school has made
important changes for
people in wheelchairs.
A cement ramp zigzags
up and around the stairs,
and I can wheel
myself to the top.

A special silver button is on the wall outside. When I push it, the front doors open and I can wheel myself inside. I can roll down the hallway to the classrooms and go through the rooms' doorways.

I can get a drink of water all by myself from the water fountain. It's just the right height for people in wheelchairs. I can wash my hands at the lower sink and I can even get in the large bathroom stall. It has a wide door that opens out so my wheelchair and I can fit inside.

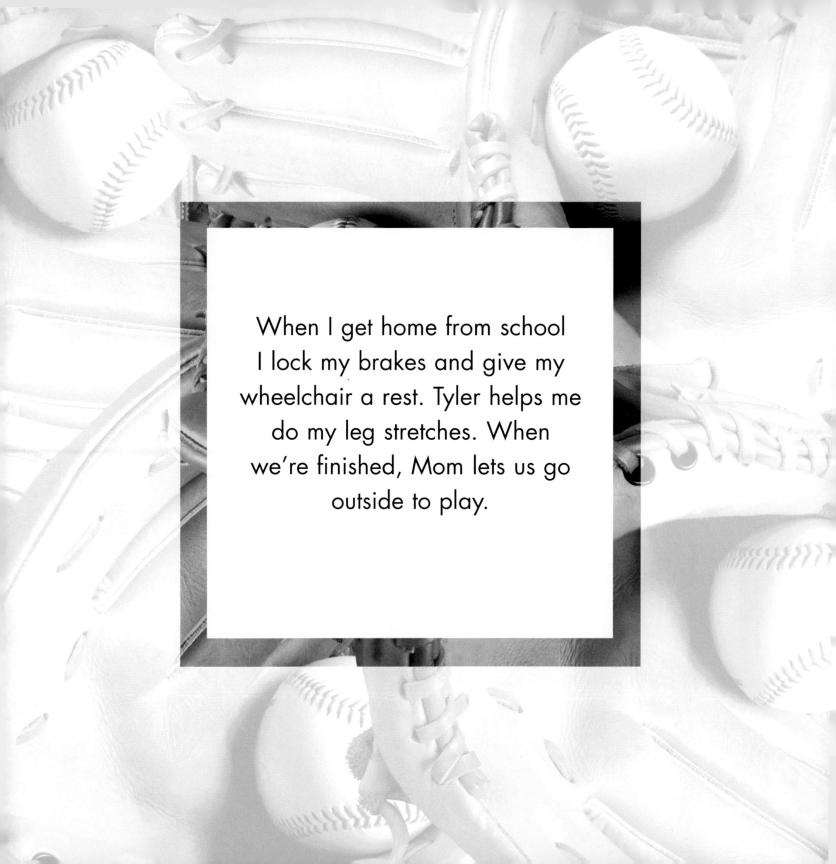

When I get home from school I lock my brakes and give my wheelchair a rest. Tyler helps me do my leg stretches. When we're finished, Mom lets us go outside to play.

My wheelchair lets me do a lot, like play all kinds of different sports with Tyler. Our favorite is basketball. Tyler runs on his two feet and does a layup. I push and steer my wheelchair with one hand and dribble the ball with my other hand. I roll as quickly as I can to the basket in my wheelchair and use both hands to shoot. It's hard, but I'm getting better and better. Sometimes I score as many points as Tyler.

My wheelchair helps me go more places on my own and do more of the things I want to do. Now nothing can stop me.